WHAT IS PROGRAMMING?

A HARMONY OF PEOPLE. CODE THAT RUNS THE WORLD. AND THE INDIVIDUAL BEHIND THE KEYBOARD.

EDAQA MORTORAY

INTRODUCTION

Everyday life is like programming, I guess. If you love something you can put beauty into it.

— DONALD KNUTH

ave you ever wondered, "What is programming?"

I don't think the answer is by any means obvious. Programming is a term bandied about, describing any number of activities in the tech world. We see two people, ostensibly both programmers, working on entirely different types of projects. We go online and see a wide range of opinions on what we thought were simple topics. And few people even have the title "Programmer" on their business card. What's going on?

My goal with this book is to show the myriad of things that a programmer does. I'm interested in looking at the profession from all angles. Many of those you may not be familiar with, and that's okay. If one quality defines programming, it's learning. From the first line of code you write, you will be adapting and discovering new things. Being sedentary is not an option.

Software is the nervous system of our world. Our society is built from millions of bits of hardware, working together to control everything we do. The internet ushered in an unavoidable information age that is reshaping our culture. Whether you find this good or bad, depends a lot on small details of the software that holds it all together.

At the forefront is basic communication. Our telephone calls, our emails, the routing of traditional mail, chatting, and the waves of social media, are all anchored in software. This places a significant level of control in the hands of people who write that software: the programmers. Daily questions about governance and morality end up being answered by lines of code. It seems prudent that we have a good idea about what programmers do. Especially if you're a programmer yourself.

Despite it permeating society, the creation of software is still shrouded in mystery. There's no definitive plan one can follow to create a successful product. Solving real-world problems is not straightforward. We often end up with the wrong solution or one that doesn't work correctly. By looking at all aspects of programming, we can better understand the troubles in the current landscape, and how to resolve them.

This book is suitable for programmers and non-programmers alike. Though I will be writing from the point of view that you are a programmer. I'll keep the level of detail approachable enough for any interested person. Programmers don't exist in a vacuum. It's vital that the teams we work with understand what we're doing.

There are many skills a programmer should learn. I take the view that all of them, over time, can be acquired through practice and study. While some people may have helpful innate abilities, great programmers are those with a growth mindset.

When I started listing all the skills, I noticed some patterns. I was able to group the skills into three broad categories. A good programmer isn't one who targets just one category but has a balance of all three.

These are the three skill categories of a programmer:

- **People** - People are the reason software exists. Software is built by people, for people. How do we figure out what all these people want, and how do we organize them to get something done? This section introduces the user, and the forms of communication needed to develop software.

- **Code** - At the heart of any software is its source code. It is the most tangible part of the product. A healthy product requires clean code. This section looks at the diverse set of technical skills and theoretical knowledge needed to write good code.
- **You** - Behind the screen is a real person: you. There are many challenges you need to overcome to excel in this profession. Programming can be an immensely rewarding activity but also bears a heavy burden. This section deals with getting ahead and remaining healthy.

ANALOGY

We can compare software to a tree.

The beautiful canopy, with all the leaves and the delicious fruit, that's what people really want. Without it, people are not interested in the tree. This is the people part of the software. We need to understand what people want in order to grow a tree they're interested in.

Those leaves and the fruit are attached to the branches, which in turn, are connected to the trunk. This is the support system. It's what holds the tree together and provides the foundation for the fruit. In our analogy, this refers to the code. Code is what holds everything together. There can be no software without code, as there can be no tree without branches.

Deeper down we have the roots, an often overlooked component. They literally give life to the tree. Any trouble with the roots will show symptoms in the branches and the bushy foliage. In software, the roots are the programmers. This is you. We can't expect to build a reliable product without strong developers.

In this book, I'm looking at the whole tree. This offers the best opportunity for growth.

MY BACKGROUND

Life is an adventure, it's not a package tour.

— ECKHART TOLLE

*M*any of you know me from my online presence. I'm a regular blogger and have been active on numerous social sites. But let me paint a more detailed picture.

I've been programming professionally for over twenty years now. In that time, I've done stints at big companies, ridden along with rocky startups, and braved the freelance world. I've been a team member, a team leader, and a department head. I've also had extensive experience interviewing and hiring developers. I've had numerous side projects and even created a programming language (technically more than one, but I'm choosing to ignore some).

My professional start was at a Canadian startup, developing tools for creating and managing websites. It's not surprising, given the role the web has taken in our society, that I'd return to it many times in my career.

An American company drew me away from my roots, pulling me to Texas for a few months, then sending me off to France. There were some great times, and a lot of flights, the last of which landed me in Germany.

In Germany, I became the head of quality assurance at an email provider. I gained insight into the whole development process. A lot of my work was in automation - not just testing, but simplifying project management and improving high-level process pipelines. Working across departments to provide a quality service was a fantastic goal.

Eventually, I found myself drawn back to the US, to an investment firm in Chicago. This was the start of my remote working career. I remained mostly in Munich and travelled several times to the US for meetings. I was one of the core developers of a high-frequency trading system. For this type of application, we needed to extract every bit of performance possible, which meant delving deep into the inner workings of the hardware and OS.

After that I worked for a Norwegian startup on a cross-platform mobile development framework -- still working remotely, but with some snowy Northern visits. I was the lead developer for the UI engine. This included writing a custom layout engine, together with support for a variety of animations and transitions. Here I finally got to address all the problems I'd had with UI development over the years. We created an excellent layout and animation system for mobile development.

While I mostly had a day job, I think I always had at least one side project and filled the gaps between jobs with other ventures. I'm a bit of a technology nomad, and I like exploring. It's unfortunate, but many of the projects I've worked on have faded away. Dealing with such things, especially when working for startups is an occupational hazard. It's a bit heartbreaking at times, but I managed to learn a great deal and had some wonderful experiences.

It's not all been technology. As my job life was starting, I ran one of the first online music magazines. That's perhaps what led me to work on web software. Continuing the music trend, I attempted a music label at one point. We released four albums, two of my own. A further and more extreme contrast was learning Lomi Lomi massage, and opening a small practice.

And of course, I've enjoyed doing lots of writing, perhaps as constant in my life as the programming. This makes it no surprise that I find myself writing this book now. Though, of course, one thing wouldn't be enough, so I've also started a food blog as well!

By no means do I know it all, but I've certainly had an extensive variety of experience. Let's hope I can share my insights and adventures with you.

WORLD OF PROGRAMMING

Exploring the unknown requires tolerating uncertainty.

— BRIAN GREENE

*M*any of you came to programming with a job in mind. You wanted to build a website for a local business. Or you wanted to create a mobile app to track their orders. The majority of modern software is specialized for one company, and your opportunity to work on generic tools is limited. Business software development touches only small portions of the world of programming, making the path to becoming a better programmer unclear.

Some of you may have come to programming out of curiosity. You started tinkering with your machine at home, creating little robots, or writing games. Your view of programming may be highly technical, without a lot of team input. If you pursue it further, you'll likely end up in a job, just like everybody else. You'll have a different insight, but still, a lot of room to grow.

Growth is a tricky thing. Everybody has a different idea of where they want to go. Things that I find interesting may not entice you at all. Topics you found interesting at the start of your career may be growing dull. Perhaps there are topics which would exhilarate you, but you just don't know about. That's why with this book, I want to touch a bit on everything and stick to topics everybody can use. I want to reassure you that you're on the right path, and also open new doors.

And there are a seemingly endless number of doors to open. As all things now have software, you can pick any industry you want. Maybe you like traditional desktop software development, or you want to design drive systems for cars. Choose one of the countless programming jobs in medical research, or the more business focused big data analysis. Do you prefer politics, or humanitarian organizations? No problem, there is always a role for a programmer.

The types of opportunities vary also. Front-end development can be appealing to those with a taste for aesthetics and user interfaces. If mathematics is your thing, there's plenty of scientific research, financial automation, or even modern game engines. Maybe you wish to venture into machine learning and artificial intelligence. Don't be afraid to hop around and try new things.

While this variety is great for you, it can lead to a few problems. Many businesses fail to understand the role programmers play. They know they need them, but aren't sure of how they fit, especially in traditionally non-technical organizations. In turn, programmers often suffer under the image they're given, and software falters from cramped approaches to development. I'd like this book to counter numerous stereotypes and misconceptions.

I'd like to give you an avenue to further explore, and develop a deeper understanding of what programming is. Whether you're just starting out in your career, or been at it for a while, I hope you'll find my writings useful. Even if you're not a programmer, reading this book will improve your understanding. You'll see that I apply the word "developer" liberally, to all those working in a software company. And it makes sense to understand how it works.

I intend on answering the questions "What is programming?" and

"What does it mean to be a programmer?". In this book, I give an overview of many aspects of the field. In further books I'll dive deeper into each one, providing a practical guide to implementation.

Please tell me your preferences for which books come next.

edaqa.com/read/programming

People

It is impossible to work in information technology without also engaging in social engineering.

— JARON LANIER

*P*rogramming is about people. You've probably heard this before. There's no way around it. If you wish to become a successful programmer you need to learn how to work with people.

I'm starting with this topic as it's often overlooked by many new to the industry. It's an area that a lot of education seems to ignore, or only cover briefly. A high number of projects fail due to a lack of communication, and misunderstanding the users. Projects that treat programming as an isolated activity have a high risk of failure.

People are not the only part of programming though. I've heard that statement made before and it's not true. They are an essential part. But that other big topic I have, called "Code," is just as vital. All these people skills are to ensure you'll be writing the correct code. The technology is also your anchor when talking with people. It's the viewpoint you represent.

In this chapter we'll look at these things:

- Understanding the user of your product, who they are, and what they want
- What a use-case is
- Non-functional requirements that users expect in a product
- Who are developers and how to create inclusive companies
- What an issue is and how it helps in project management
- How to prioritize with risk and value assessment
- The difficulty of timelines and estimation
- Getting feedback from non-programmers
- Your role as the arbiter of technical concerns

THE USER

The most important property of a program is whether it accomplishes the intention of its user.

— C.A.R. HOARE

Thinking that programming is about programmers is the worst mistake you can make. The single most important aspect of programming is the user. Keep this in mind through all the discussions we have, even down to the lowest technical details of an operating system. The only reason we need programming is for users.

Who is the user? As they are the people we ultimately serve, we need to understand who they are, and who they aren't. In the most abstract sense, a user is anybody using technology to accomplish a goal.

It's the photographer touching up their photos. It's a gamer relaxing behind a controller. It's friends talking to each other on the phone. It's an accountant entering numbers into a spreadsheet. It's the thousands of people browsing social media, or the few organizing a weekend getaway. It's a hungry man ordering a burger late Saturday night. It's a musician putting the final touches on their new master-piece. It's the medical researcher trying to create a new vaccine.

The list focuses on people doing real things. I've intentionally omitted a lot of what I consider to be secondary users. These are people producing tools for other people to serve end users. These are the administrators and programmers who use technology and libraries. We're users, but a special category. Our requirements need to be met, but ultimately we need to cater to the primary user.

Note that I haven't mentioned software here. A user doesn't care about software, hardware, or anything in between. The user has a high-level, real-world task. Many components need to work together to help them. Thinking about the hardware, software, and process separately does a disservice to the user.

Ideally, the user's thoughts never leave their application domain. They shed no worry about the bits they are using, blending them seamlessly into their life. One approach here is to create a persona. Define a fictional person, their name, their job, where they live, and everything they do. Provide a flow for this person by trying to be part of their life. We need empathy to understand their problems. Any time we make a decision, we must consider the impact it has on those users. Frustration arises from mismatches in expectations, not neces-sarily defects.

Furthermore, we need to consider what abilities our user has. They aren't as computer literate as us -- again, their thoughts ideally don't need to leave their domain. Getting into the user's head lets us use terms, symbols, and processes they will understand. The user shouldn't have to read this book to use the tools we make.

Way beyond knowledge, not all humans are created the same. Not just disabilities, but minor variations, like finger size, can make applications hard to use. We don't all have the same reaction time, nor the same appreciation of, or even ability to distinguish colours. In a world where everything is connected, we have to consider all people. Leaving even a few behind is unfair.

Creating good software requires understanding our users. Who are they? What are they capable of? What do they want to do? This goes well outside the realm of programming, to all development teams. There is only one reason why we develop software, and it needs to be at the forefront of our thoughts, always.

The user.

USER STORIES AND REQUIREMENTS

The user's going to pick dancing pigs over security every time.

— BRUCE SCHNEIER

*A*lthough I just said we must think like the user, we can't do that all the time. If we don't also think like a programmer, nothing will get done. This means we need a way to capture what the user wants. That is, while thinking like a user, we write down what is required, then switch to thinking like a programmer.

Generally, we start from a broad picture of the user. From here we work our way down into specific activities. We isolate a useful sequence of actions. For example, a photographer wants to browse the photos on their camera. The accountant wants to reconcile their bank statement.

These high-level scenarios are known as user stories.

From these user stories, we can determine what the system has to do. We define the interactions, components, and behaviours that specifically fulfill a user story. We call these the functional require-ments, and we often capture these concrete requirements in use-cases. Where the story is the primary value proposition, the use-case is how we'll achieve it.

Without the functional requirements, the technology has no value to the user.

But use-cases are only a fraction of the overall requirements of a system. There a large number of implied expectations from the users, as well as the needs of the developers and administrators. Beyond technical needs, we have a variety of financial and legal obligations that software might need to fulfill.

As everything is now online, security and privacy are significant issues. The users expect their information to be safe and secure by default. It's not something they expect to have to configure. Different countries have distinct requirements for how data is handled. Your marketing department also has wishes and desires of data. There are a lot of potentially conflicting requirements that need to be balanced.

Software is a living entity. We don't create it once and move on. We continually add new features and fix bugs. Maintenance is a significant non-functional requirement. Can we track versions of the software? Can we ensure that new features don't break old ones? Can we upgrade the servers with new versions?

The list of requirements goes well beyond the simple things a user wants to do. All the requirements that don't directly support a use-case are considered non-functional requirements.

As with all terms in this book, don't get too caught up in the specific meanings. It's a blurry line between functional and non-functional requirements. As long as we recognize that both are required, it's not vital that each requirement is classified correctly.

THE "DEVELOPER"

To make a rock'n'roll record, technology is the least important thing.

— KEITH RICHARDS

I give the title "developer" to everybody in a software company. Why should a programmer be considered a developer any more than the person doing community management? Why does the code hold more value than a sales strategy about getting that code in the hands of users? The graphic team's UI animations are an essential part of the software. The tester verifies requirements and provides feedback to improve the overall quality. Account managers are on the front line of understanding what the clients want.

This list goes on and on. We have no problem saying a company develops software, so why don't we refer to its employees as developers? Calling only programmers "developers" diminishes the importance of all those other roles. It may seem like a trivial detail, but these small things leave lasting impressions. They change how we think about development, and how we interact as teams.

If you're familiar with the Scrum method, you might be thinking about cross-functional teams now. Ideas of horizontal integration across a company come up in any process or discussion of quality and management. We may not know for sure what the best approach is, but there's no doubt we need to get all developers working together.

And for us? We have the term "programmer" that says who we are. A lot of the development responsibility ultimately falls on us. The better we can balance the wishes of all developers, the better the software will perform for everybody.

I know there's a constant fight for better sounding job titles. It's a futile, even counterproductive battle. We see terms like "software architect" appear, even though it's not a distinct role from programming. Unfortunately though, once the title appears, somebody will try to fulfill that role specifically. We end up with over-specialization and responsibility dilution.

I'll mostly ignore all the fancy titles. I'll talk about "coding," "programming" and "developing."

PROJECT MANAGEMENT

Success in management requires learning as fast as the world is changing.

— WARREN BENNIS

*W*e've seen that a lot of people contribute to the development of software. Even for small teams, there are many ideas and requirements floating around. Every stakeholder, everybody with some interest in the project, is an active part of an evolving plan.

Project management has come a long way since the start of programming, where an atrocious waterfall model once ruled. That evolved into more adaptive systems, which recognized the need for more flexibility. These progressed further into the agile methods we see today, such as lean programming or Scrum. It isn't stopping here either. The state of affairs in software development methods is under constant flux.

Why is that? It's because of change. We're continually looking for better ways to deal with evolving requirements.

While everything that needs to be done may seem clear during a kick-off meeting, it won't take long for the first issue to appear. By the second day, opinions will change. By the end of the week, somebody will be demanding timelines. These are actually good signs. A project where nothing changes implies the stakeholders have lost interest.

We need a way to manage the development of software, organize all these people. This management needs to happen across teams and within teams. Not all this work falls on the programmer of course. As companies grow beyond a few individuals, there will be a project manager, and possibly a distinct product manager. They won't usually be programmers or even necessarily have a programming background, but it's vital to have a proper way to communicate the goals and progress of the project.

That's a lot of avenues to look at. No wonder we haven't agreed upon one approach to development. Don't think this means it's okay not to follow a method. While you don't need to stick rigorously to a defined process, it'd be foolish to ignore the tried and true practices they have created.

I'm also not saying the system has to appear overnight. There's nothing wrong with starting small, using a spreadsheet, or a Kanban board on the wall. You may also come into a chaotic environment, and need to set something up at least for yourself. Full project management systems grow over time from small beginnings.

ISSUES

Quality is everyone's responsibility.

— W. EDWARDS DEMING

*L*et's take a look at the most specific tracking system first: the issue system.

There's a lot of words for issues: defects, bugs, features, enhancements, wishes, errors, tasks, the list goes on and on. Don't get lost trying to differentiate these terms. I prefer to use "issue" as the generic word. It encompasses the widest range and has the least potential to cause arguments. I've seen arguments arise over the difference between defects and wishes before. One person's severe defect is another person's low priority feature request.

An issue is a mismatch between behaviour and expectations. This is intentionally a broad definition. It's the one you should be using. And you'll need an issue system to keep a log of them. Here you'll record everything, from feature requests to defects, to potential refactoring ideas.

Initially, it's not even essential to record what type an issue is. As I said, it's easy to disagree on whether something is broken or by design

-- it can also be both. The goal of an issue is to collect the viewpoints, the details, and arrive at a suitable prioritization. Letting an arbitrary label play a significant role is not a good idea. An issue needs to be evaluated based on properties like severity, frequency, and value.

Consider accounting software. An issue comes in that exported PDF invoices sometimes have odd lines on the edges. That sounds like a defect. You'd better fix it. Another small issue comes in requesting a second sales tax field. Oh well, that's a feature request, we don't have time for both, and we'd better prioritize defects first. Two weeks later, the account manager is happy the invoices are fixed. Of course, sales is quite upset that they'll be unable to sell the product in regions that require a second tax. This doesn't sound like it has a high-value outcome.

Looking at critical systems is another good way to demonstrate the necessity of in-depth evaluation of issues. Let's say we're developing an autonomous vehicle. An issue is logged: whenever the car comes to a complete stop the music playback stutters slightly. This is a high-frequency issue. It's going to happen all the time, and probably easy to debug.

Meanwhile, another issue surfaces: in two tests the car failed to come to a complete stop at a stop sign. It's rare. Of 20,000 logged stops it's only happened twice. This is going to be hard to debug.

The audio issue has a relatively low severity. It will annoy the passengers, and probably be mentioned in reviews of the car. The failing-to-stop issue has an extreme severity. It can result in a crash, potentially with injuries and loss of life. 1 in 10,000 may sound rare, but it's going to happen frequently when deployed to thousands of drivers.

The role of issue management is to balance the desires of a project with the available resources. This is essentially project management at a more detailed lower level.

PRIORITIZATION, RISK, VALUE

If you don't actively attack the risks, the risks will actively attack you.

— TOM GILB

*T*here's too much to do. There will always be too much to do.

As software develops, so does the list of issues associated with it. These are the defects, feature requests, oddities, enhancements and any change that needs to be made. This will be for the user, the admins, the sales team, the programmers, or any other team involved.

There won't be time to do them all.

Yet everyone will consider their issue as essential to their work. To avoid stress and tension, we need to work as a unified development team. This is a strong motivator to call everybody in the company a developer. If any team's requests are seen as less valid than others, you'll end up with fights. Instead of discussions of priorities, you can end up with accusations of ignorance and selfishness.

Having a transparent issue system can go a long way to assuage tensions.

Once we have the issues tracked, we need a way to order them.

Prioritization should not be done ad hoc, as it results in missing out on valuable opportunities and underused time. On the flip-side, an overly detailed process results in a backlog of unprocessed issues. It also costs a lot of time, something which is in short supply.

The balance between precision and speed leads to an attribute-based system. Issues are labeled with severity for defects, and value for features. Each issue is assigned a rough time estimation cost. Flags are added for issues affecting vital customers, or prominent marketing features. A regression flag is common when backwards compatibility is critical.

All attributes should be reasonably objective. Even something like value should be based on some concrete sales goals. The values don't always need to be correct. It's natural that mistakes will be made. But we're looking for a balance. Additionally, being objective means others can review the values.

From these attributes, a priority is assigned to an issue. This is based on a combination of risk, intuition, and preference.

Risk is a tricky subject. It's a subjective estimate of how damage can be done to the company if the issue is not resolved. It's the negative counterpart to value. Value is the subjective estimate of how much value can be brought to the company. We could combine value and risk into an impact score. Issues with a high impact should be given a high priority. As the impact score drops, so does the priority.

We can't discount intuition here. As we aren't doing a detailed analysis, there are inevitably some aspects lost. If any developer speaks for an issue, it makes sense to listen. A certain amount of time should be dedicated to the issues that just feel like priority targets, even if the attributes don't overtly justify it.

Programmer preference must also be considered. We aren't machines. Priority has no correlation with interest. If week after week I work on nothing but boring, or frustrating, issues, I will get stressed, and my productivity will drop. Picking our own issues helps with motivation. It makes us feel more attached to the project.

There's no shortage of complexity in prioritization. It's the linchpin of successful development. It doesn't matter how good your developers are if you can't figure out what to work on. It's no wonder that it plays a central role in most processes, and that an endless number of books have been written about it. Thus, there's plenty of opinions and ideas to debate.

If you want to take away just one point now, it's that prioritization must be done. It is not optional. This means making hard choices about what is important, what must be done now, and what will be tossed aside. An unwillingness to prioritize is the surest way to get nothing done. This leads us into our next section.

ESTIMATION AND TIMELINES

Good software, like wine, takes time.

— JOEL SPOLSKY

*T*here's never enough time to do it all, yet something has to get done. Ultimately the investors want to see results. In turn, management wants to see progress. We've entered the land of estimations and timelines.

It's reasonable that a business wants to plan their products. The whole company needs to be organized. Things unrelated from coding must be set in motion to ensure everything is ready on time.

Yet, timelines remain a delicate subject.

Not all issues can be realistically estimated. An experienced programmer may be able to give a rough estimate to some features, but it'll have a lot of variation. Some defects defy any ability to predict, even after working on them for a while.

It's great when a complex issue turns out to be something simple. It's bad when a simple problem turns out to require a substantial change in how the product works. It's awful when after days of debugging nobody can figure out the cause of a high-risk defect.

A planning process must consider this uncertainty. Otherwise, it is broken. This may sound obvious, but there are a lot of broken processes out there. Treating an estimate as a guaranteed timeframe invites many troubles. Yet time and again, programmers are requested to give detailed, precise estimates, and then held to them.

Fortunately, over the past decades, we've developed many ways to plan with uncertainty. Agile software development is one of the umbrella terms used. You'll also hear about continuous delivery, where we strive to always have a shippable product. We may even start from a walking skeleton: a minimal system that works end-to-end but is lacking in many ways. From there we can build a minimum viable product (MVP).

We can still use estimates, but we recognize their limitations. We stop focusing on well-defined packages of features. Instead, we focus on a working product with continual improvements. Never are we left in a situation where we have nothing new, or a broken product.

This, at a glance, may sound like simply not planning, but to be effective, we have to balance our options. We can try a mixture of flexible deadlines and flexible feature sets. Which is more important depends a lot on the project. But in no case can you fix both the features and deadlines. That's a recipe for disappointment.

Regardless of which approach is chosen, all developers must be on board. From the management through to the programmers. Everybody must understand the process.

NON-PROGRAMMERS ARE COMPUTER USERS

Each new user of a new system uncovers a new class of bugs.

— BRIAN W. KERNIGHAN

*L*et's think again about who I call a developer: everybody working in a software development company. I also said the user is the most important person. We all work to serve the user. I keep stressing the need to work with all of these people. Now, I'm going to take it one step beyond this.

Users are not programmers, but they are an essential part of the development process. They use software and hardware every day. They know and interact with other people. The users work in companies with issues systems, facing similar problems to yours. They all have insights and ideas.

You, as a programmer, are rarely the target demographic for your product. Even when you are, you're but a single user with a single desire. Despite how close you are to the technology, you are not the expert in the user's domain. You're also not a marketing person, an accountant, or anything else like that.

So, if somebody wants to talk, listen!

A lot of valuable information comes from idle conversations with users, and other non-programming developers. From ideas about how the product could be used to insight into planning features. Maybe nothing new comes from it. But instead of pushing away an interested person, you've brought somebody closer to the project. This does wonders for motivation within the company. It also makes users in your burgeoning community feel special.

By talking about what you're developing, you gain a better insight into what you're doing. There's a concept called "rubber duck coding," where you literally talk to a rubber duck on your desk. It's a known approach to work through problems. Well, guess what? Talking to random people can do the same thing.

Don't wait, ask for input. As conversation is valuable, it makes sense to encourage it. Give the users a feedback button, or a way to ask for help. They'll appreciate it, even if they don't use it.

Far too often technical issues are dismissed as too complicated for "average" people. This is utter nonsense. Look at what everybody is doing with technology, their phones, TVs, home automation, their cars, or just about everything. They may not understand things in the same terms as programmers, but it'd be wrong to assume they don't understand. Attempting to communicate problems we're having is an excellent exercise for ourselves.

Sure, inevitably you have the types that want to contribute too much. We'll have to talk about them more eventually. But perhaps books on psychology are better suited to the task. Fortunately, few people are like this.

THE ULTIMATE JUDGE OF CODE
MATTERS

In programming, the hard part isn't solving problems, but deciding
what problems to solve.

— PAUL GRAHAM

All this talk of other developers and users may leave you
questioning what your role actually is. I'd like to stress that
communication with these people is a primary part of your position.
It may seem like anybody can do this function, or even that it doesn't
describe any role at all. How is what I described different from a
project manager?

It's about viewpoint and responsibility.

I've talked about a lot of things now. Many things that don't seem
related to source code, the place where you feel most comfortable.
And don't worry at all, I'll get to the code. We'll discuss it thoroughly.
But there's a reason I've gone into the people angle first. To be a
successful programmer, to be a successful coder, you need to understand the reason for your work. Without the framework of the business, without the user, without those other developers, you can't be
successful at your job.

Your role, however, is not a project manager. You represent the technical side of this equation. Programmers are expected to understand the technical risks and value propositions. This is your area of expertise, and it's crucial that you communicate your opinion. Prioritization done without this input will be seriously flawed.

It's essential you follow the prioritization as well. Ultimately the individual teams decide which issues they work on. Working on the wrong things disrupts planning, discredits the programmers, and creates frustration.

Yet, a lot of your time will be self-directed. Precisely how you do your work is your decision. There a numerous ways to fulfill requirements. There are plenty of ways to spend our time. Nobody should be micro-managing you. This leaves a great deal of responsibility on your shoulders. Take all the knowledge you've gained, and apply it to your work.

SOCIAL SKILLS

The advance of technology is based on making it fit in so that you don't really even notice it, so it's part of everyday life.

— BILL GATES

*P*rogramming is about people. If you want to truly understand development, you need to talk with all the people involved in this field. If you're interested in getting ahead, you need to see your work from a variety of viewpoints.

Communication is an immense task, but don't worry, it doesn't all fall on your shoulders. You'll be part of a team. Not everybody needs to do everything. As long as you coordinate, you can divide responsibility. Of course, this implies social skills are vital even within the programming team. There's no way to get away from that.

The stereotype of a lone coder locked away in a dark room has always been wrong. There are plenty of times when it may be productive to code alone, but those are isolated. If you're spending days out of contact with team members, and other teams, then you're doing something wrong. Even if you have a complicated technical milestone, you still need to keep your team abreast of your progress.

Your worth as a programmer is viewed through how you communicate with others. Code mastery is irrelevant if there is nobody to appreciate it. Other developers don't want to talk about code, they want to talk about how that code serves the user and their own needs. They want to share a vision of a product with you. Demonstrating your understanding, and accepting them as part of the team, improves your perceived worth. It has the nice side effect of improving the product quality as well.

This doesn't mean you must be a smooth-talking, charismatic leader. Social skills, like coding skills, are something that can be learned and improved upon over time. The key is a willingness to work on these abilities. It's not enough to focus on code alone. Your career will be stunted if your social, and project management, skills don't grow as well.

Code

Coding is extremely creative and is an integral part of almost every industry.

— RESHMA SAUJANI

*C*ode is what many people envision when they think of programming. It's the glue holding everything together.

As much as it's not the goal of programming to produce code, code plays the most central role. How we approach writing code, and the quality of it, are significant factors in the success of the project.

In this section I'll look at the approaches to coding. I've split it roughly between the theoretical foundation and practical aspects. But this is only an organization device for the book, with a few exceptions, you can't really do one without the other.

Code has a lot of facets. It's important to inspect all of them.

PART I
THEORY

A lot of coding knowledge transcends the code itself.

Theory is an attempt to collect this abstract knowledge about coding. We attempt to find forms, and approaches, that can survive beyond a project, and hopefully, many years to come. We're looking to solve classes of problems, rather than instances of them.

In this section we'll:

- Consider the diverse range of opinions in our field
- Examine fundamentally different strategies to coding known as paradigms
- Learn how patterns help us code
- Expand on non-functional requirements, those things a system must do, but aren't the reason it exists
- Determine what an algorithm is, how to use them, and how to create them
- Look briefly at how we measure algorithms with complexity theory
- Get a teaser about the deep thoughts of type theory

DIVERSE OPINIONS

The amateur software engineer is always in search of magic.

— GRADY BOOCH

*F*irst, I need to give a significant warning: there are diverse opinions on the correct way to code. There's no definitive approach to writing clean code or discovering the best architecture. Each library may appear to have a different interface and may be riding a new trend. Legacy and infant projects often seem vastly different. Forums are full of people arguing.

Don't let that variety mislead you into thinking there is no commonality. There is a large amount of standard process and known techniques that lead to solid code.

For example, while it's easy to argue about what precisely clean code is or how much time we dedicate to refactoring, there is no question about the value of clean code itself. Any articles you find online saying otherwise can be safely discarded as nonsense.

Another example is with version control. We argue about optimal branching strategy. We debate how code reviews should be done. We can argue whether GIT, Bazaar or Mercurial is better. But there's no question that branching, merging, and version management are an essential part of modern programming.

The lack of consensus makes education an interesting question. Worse, what's considered standard is still changing quickly. Many curriculums have gotten left behind. Whether your local school teaches you the skills you need has a lot to do with luck and timing.

This may be why degrees and certifications are not required in this field, and why they have less value than in others. Though, it'd be silly to say that they're worthless. Given the amount there is to learn, you can't really go wrong learning something. There's no guarantee it'll be enough. We can more fairly make the opposite guarantee: it won't be enough.

Perhaps more challenging are the numerous bad articles online. Many people of limited experience ride the wave of diverse opinions and publish things that are wrong. While much of the nonsense may be evident to some, it's a different story if you're new to programming. Hopefully, my writing can also serve as a yardstick to measure the legitimacy of such coding tips.

PARADIGMS

I find languages that support just one programming paradigm constraining.

— BJARNE STROUSTRUP

There's more than one type of source code, as there's more than one way to tell the computer what to do. Drawing rough distinctions between the various approaches is possible. We call the different approaches paradigms. By learning them, we gain new ideas on how to solve problems. We learn about more succinct and accurate ways to express our requirements.

You'll find these paradigms are argued about online. Different camps will promote some paradigms as superior, but the truth is that each of the paradigms has its strengths and weaknesses. It depends on context which one is better to use. You should learn all of them. Otherwise, you will use the wrong one.

These are a few commonly used paradigms: Imperative, functional, event, reactive, and declarative. I'll describe each of them now briefly, with a few advantages and disadvantages of each. These are not meant to be seen as definitive dividing classes, but more as a collection of concepts. Actual code will blend the different approaches.

Imperative code, often called procedural programming, it's a series of statements, with branches and functions, and variables. One thing happens after another. As a coder, we specify what happens, when, and how. Its primary advantage is that it's how computers basically work. It models workflow well and can be easy to read. Its disadvantage is the requirement to strictly handle many conditions and the difficulty in verifying its correctness.

Object-oriented programming is a type of imperative coding. Its concepts have become familiar enough that we often don't see it as a distinct paradigm -- unless you see code that doesn't use it, where its absence is wholly noticeable. Its focus is primarily on the distinction between data and operations on the data. It takes a data-type centric view of the world, offering features like encapsulation and polymorphism.

Functional coding has a more mathematical view to its thinking. It deals with transformations of data through expressions. It doesn't have any side-effects, making it exceptionally safe, simple to optimize, and easy to run concurrently. But it doesn't model multi-step processes, or external interactions, well. We often see it used for pure calculations, algorithms that deal mainly with CPU. It's rare to see imperative code that doesn't include functional components.

Event coding is a paradigm that focuses on connecting components together. One module publishes an event, and other modules respond via listeners. It's an asynchronous model that provides excellent separation of responsibility yet still allows several components to work together. It has to be used with another paradigm since, on their own, events don't get work done.

Reactive coding is a paradigm that creates permanent relationships between values. Rather than one-time calculations, a reactive expression updates its result whenever the source value changes. Perhaps first popularized in spreadsheets, and seen commonly in stream form for audio processing, it's now become a valued tool in user interface programming and other feedback systems. It's sometimes called functional reactive, though, in practice, reactive coding without the functional aspect is rather useless.

There's an overlap between the event and reactive paradigms, as there is between many of them. We could view reactive programming as a form of filtered event coding: change events are broadcast and handled by several listeners. This is how it is often implemented. It serves a specialized purpose though, and often paradigms may be separated primarily by the use they serve, as opposed to just their form.

Let's not leave out declarative programming. It is a paradigm that expresses the desired result, not how to achieve it. It uses rules and constraints to describe a user interface, the layout of a network, the structure of a document, or a language parser. It's interesting that declarative languages can work in different directions: an HTML document says how to compose a specific document, whereas a regular expression is used to decompose any number of strings. Declarative languages are highly domain specific, offering a concise syntax for those applications.

Unfortunately, many people don't consider some paradigms to be proper coding. For example, because writing an HTML document doesn't feel like writing a device driver, it's often cast aside and treated as a second class citizen. Note, I'm using the term coding here. With my definition of programming, it would be ridiculous to exclude any of these paradigms. But I see no reason why they aren't all considered coding anyway. Choosing the right approach to coding is essential to being a productive programmer. There is no hierarchy of "better" and "worse" paradigms, only the right tool for a particular job.

I've given you only a brief glimpse at paradigms here. I want to introduce you to the concept. It's a topic that deserves to have it's own book to explore fully. There is so much more to say, and so many more paradigms to cover.

Instead of being tools, paradigms are a whole toolbox. They provide entirely different ways to approach a problem. Knowing how to use these different approaches makes you a well-rounded programmer.

PATTERNS

"Sometimes, the elegant implementation is just a function. Not a method. Not a class. Not a framework. Just a function." - John Carmack

$\mathcal{I}$f we say that paradigms are coding strategies, then patterns are the tactics. Patterns are specific structures of code well suited to a particular task. They're a set of blueprints, ready to be called upon when we need to build some code.

Many collections of patterns have been written, perhaps popularized through object-oriented programming. You'll find names and descriptions of use. Not all of the names will have wide-spread use, though there are common ones like interfaces and adapters. As part of the running theme, not all the names have universally accepted meaning. It's therefore essential to understand what the pattern describes, and what it's good for.

There are no one-size-fits-all patterns. Every application of a pattern will be distinct. There is no need to implement a pattern precisely as described in a book, though they can be good starting points. Unlike algorithms, which provide a specific data transformation, patterns are used to hold code together. The pattern itself isn't an end goal. It's scaffolding.

The variation in implementation is perhaps why we don't always agree on the names. This isn't a license to throw names around at random. Using common terms, as they're often defined, helps others navigate and understand your code.

The most common patterns find their way into programming languages. Having syntactic support for things like classes, interfaces, and optional values keeps code clean.

NON-FUNCTIONAL REQUIREMENTS

Computers are useless. They can only give you answers.

— PABLO PICASSO

*Y*ou can't plant a flag at the peak, without the mountain supporting it. There's what a user wants to do, and all the things needed to ensure they can do it successfully, and safely.

When talking about the user before, we also spoke about non-functional requirements. These are all the things expected of a product but aren't the reason we use the product. They're the mountain holding up the peak. For example, we use chat programs to talk to people, the functional part and expect it to be private, the non-functional part.

Many non-functional requirements originate primarily from the technical side. We expect our system to keep running as the number of users increases. This is a scaling, or performance, requirement. If there is a crash, we'd like to keep running, and definitely don't want to lose all the data. This is a fault tolerance requirement.

I guess you could see these as expected requirements from the user as well. They don't want the system to be slow, and they don't like losing what they've written. But at the technical level, we're interested in breaking it down to a much finer level. We need to come up with actionable features that can be implemented and improved over time.

A lot of these features are the type which aren't noticed unless they go wrong. People don't notice adequate performance, they tend to only see lousy performance. As these features may lack tangible results, they can often become points of contention in the planning process. It's why risk is an essential value to consider during prioriti- zation. Without risk, many of these requirements would never be regarded as valuable.

Non-functional requirements permeate the product and aren't tied to specific components. For example, security isn't a module you can add in. All the code has to be aware of security concerns. This makes non-functional requirements tricky to implement consistently. How does one ensure that any new use-case implementation meets all the needs of security, maintenance, and scalability?

Here are some of the primary non-functional technical requirements:

- Security & Privacy: The system must be protected against unauthorized access, while allowed privileged users the tools to maintain it.
- Fault Tolerance: As components break, or fail, what is the strategy to recover operations? Which parts can automatically recover? Which need manual steps? How is data preserved?
- Scalability: How do you deal with an increasing user base, or increasing user load? Nodes can be scaled up, or the whole system scaled out. Either way, the code will likely need to be adjusted to make it possible.
- Maintainability: The product isn't ephemeral. More features are coming over time. It must be possible to keep running and adapt to changing needs.
- Legal Compliance: No product is outside of the tangle of

legal requirements. What you do with data is constrained by laws. Those laws are often in place to ensure other non-functional requirements are met, such as privacy.

Those cover some of the significant areas of non-functional requirements. They can be split further into more categories. This is something I'd like to look at more in one of my further writings. Overlooking non-functional requirements can be easy. Having a more complete list helps discover what needs to be done, it gives ideas of what could go wrong.

ALGORITHMS

Programming is one of the most difficult branches of applied mathematics; the poorer mathematicians had better remain pure mathematicians.

— EDSGER DIJKSTRA

*S*omewhere beneath all our high-level features reside a critical part of coding: algorithms. These are what sort our lists, encode our images, decide what process to run next, and implement the protocol to talk to the server. Algorithms make our computers work.

As our day-to-day work often focuses on integration and business logic, it's easy to lose track of the lowly algorithm. Our abstract languages and tools let us think primarily in the problem domain, which is marvellous. It allows us to focus on getting things done.

We can't forget algorithms are there though. They're always there. They're the heart of our software.

It's befitting of any programmer to understand what they are, how to use them, and how to create them.

WHAT

One could argue that any piece of code is an algorithm. But this isn't what comes to mind when we speak of "algorithms." Writing a precise definition has been a point of contention for many years. Thus I will rely a bit on intuition.

An algorithm is a series of steps which solves a problem. Key to this is that the steps are unambiguous and the problem is discrete. Unambiguous means the algorithm is a clearly specified set of calculations and transformations, there are no magical or abstract steps. Discrete means it exists on its own, taking a well-defined input and producing a well-defined output.

Algorithms have a defined start point, a defined endpoint, and don't wait on anything. The lack of waiting distinguishes an algorithm from software in general. An application is not an algorithm as it's long-lived and waits on input. It also streams results over time, rather than providing a discrete output. It may be a contentious definition, but I think it covers most of our intuitive feeling.

We tend to consider algorithms in a pure world. We can reason about them without needing to know their specific use. For example, we can talk about creating efficient indexes on database tables without knowing how a database stores user records. A path-finding algorithm works with nodes and edges, rather than roads and vehicles. A sorting algorithm converts an unordered list into an ordered one, whereas a sorting application deals with loading and saving the data.

In this sense, we apply algorithms to real-world problems. They are tools used to solve business problems. We consider the high-level problem to be the application, not the algorithm. Fortunately, in daily coding, the need to distinguish doesn't come up. Thus we don't need a perfect definition.

HOW

It feels like a relatively recent phenomenon that we can code without creating algorithms. At the highest levels, such as web or mobile business apps, much of the algorithm work is already done by the frameworks and libraries we're using. This is great, as it lets us focus on the problem domain. But it's also unfortunate since the world of algorithms is vibrant and exciting.

Unless you're doing something genuinely exotic, designing an algorithm is easier than it sounds. Mostly, we take an existing algorithm and adapt it to our needs. The tricky part here is knowing which algorithms you have available and picking a suitable one.

Adapting your problem to an existing algorithm is called reduction. You're reducing the form of your problem into a form that already has a solution. For example, say you wish to select the students with the top three scores from a recent test. We can instead phrase this problem as sorting the tests by score, and choosing the first three. This lets us use any of the standard sorting algorithms to solve our problem.

Should you actually need a new algorithm, there are some standard design paradigms at your disposal. These give you approaches to solving a problem in standard ways. Like code paradigms though, they are a strategy, not specific tactics.

For example, a brute force algorithm forgoes elegance and takes advantage of raw computing power. Capacity is not endless though, so to lessen the load for complex problems, we move into divide-and-conquer or dynamic programming. Many problems, especially in AI, can be formulated as searching through a tree. In some cases, like financial predictions, random sampling is effective.

I feel as though we're barely scratching the surface here. I could, and will eventually, provide a book dedicated to algorithms. The more you know about them, the better programmer you'll be. A lot of algorithm design is basic stuff. Get some experience doing it, and you'll find you use it a lot more often.

COMPLEXITY THEORY

An investment in knowledge pays the best interest.

— BENJAMIN FRANKLIN

ost programming is at a level where we don't often think about theory. This is a testament to how well we've been able to abstract and simplify technology over the past decades. Yet, the core of computing is still run by an assortment of well-studied algorithms. This evaluation is done with something called computational complexity.

The complexity of an algorithm is a measure of how many resources it uses. This could be how long it takes to run or how much memory it uses. Study of complexity has wide-ranging implications, including how efficient automated driving can be and whether encryption is secure.

Without having at least a rudimentary understanding of complexity theory, there will be something missing from your programming knowledge. You don't need to become an expert, but at least learn enough to be part of the conversation. Eventually, you'll encounter code that takes too long, and you'll want to understand why that is.

Time complexity is a good starting point. In the simplest terms, we need a way to count how many "steps" an algorithm takes.

You've probably seen things like $O(n)$ before, called "Big-O of N." It is a way to specify the maximum number of steps an algorithm takes. Summing up a list of numbers is $O(n)$: we create a loop over the values and add to a total for each one. That's n additions.

For sorting, we'll have $O(n * log(n))$. There's nothing fancy here, it's just a math expression. For example, if you had *100* items, it would take *100 * log(100) ~= 460* comparisons. I say comparisons since that's usually the slowest part of sorting, and thus the part we count.

Not all measures are created equally. In casual use, we're lenient in what we mean. This leads to a lot of confusion and potential misinformation. It's important to understand why a hash map insert that is supposed to be $O(1)$ can often take N steps. Are we justified in calling it $O(1)$? What do we need to know to make fair comparisons?

We also seem to be stuck using Big-O $O(n)$ notation, when Big-Theta $\Theta(n)$ is usually what we mean. There are several more of these symbols, and a lot of misinformation about them online. By studying complexity, the meaning behind these symbols, we gain a deeper insight into how algorithms work. This helps us select the right solution to a problem or understand why it may not be working out.

TYPE THEORY

To solve math problems, you need to know the basic mathematics before you can start applying it.

— CATHERINE ASARO

*I*f you've gone down the rabbit hole of complexity theory, you might be happy to learn there's another adventure waiting for you. Welcome to the realm of type theory.

All of us rely on type theory with every single line of code we write. You may not be actively thinking about it, but it's there.

On a daily basis, we deal with practical matters. Those expressions we write; they all have a type, such as an integer value. Classes and functions have types and specify how they transform between types. Some types can be automatically converted, others cannot. These are all rules defined in the type system of the language.

Learning the rules of the language is essential to coding in it successfully. Some of the rules will be enforced by the compiler, while others are applied at runtime. Even knowing this distinction is vital.

If you wish to venture beyond the practical matters, you can either enter the world of compilers or put on a different hat and go into the realm of math and type theory. There's a lot of overlap between the two areas of study. One leans more towards practical applications, and the other towards rigour and analysis.

Abstractly, or as a language designer, we start looking closely at what types mean. How can they be formulated? How can they be reduced? We look at what inheritance really means, and whether type conversions form consistent systems. We're interested in discovering unifying rules.

Do we really need this level of theory?

Anytime we use technology that we don't truly understand, we risk making mistakes. The push into theory is about understanding how code truly works. Many of the defects that arise in software are due to inconsistencies, or problems, at the theoretical level. The deeper we go, the more rooted our knowledge becomes. We discover new avenues to approach coding. We uncover the source of our problems.

That said, few of you will likely go down this path. It can benefit you greatly, but there's a lot to understand, and it's quite far removed from typical programming tasks.

PART II
PRACTICE

A program is like a poem: you cannot write a poem without writing it.

— E. W. DIJKSTRA

We understand the people. We know the theory. But that's not enough. The code has to be written.

It's not only about solving a problem. It's about creating a sustainable solution. It's about working within real-world limits. It's about anticipating problems without getting side-tracked by perfection.

In this section we'll cover:

- The need and value of practice
- Learning how skills transfer through ever-changing technology
- The erasure of lines between administration and coding
- Productivity and quality gains made with automation

- Managing changes to source code
- Keeping code clean and legible for future programmers
- Creating robust code
- The vital role of testing
- The value of understanding how a computer works

PRACTICE AND EXPERIMENT

Write code every day.

— JOHN RESIG

*B*ecoming a good programmer requires lots of practice. This is true of most abilities, so it's no surprise it's true of coding, and programming as a whole.

Some practice will come from sticking with a project for a long time. Long term projects have a lot of challenges that won't be found on small projects. A lot of the complexity of programming comes as a product starts to mature. The complications arise from all parts of the spectrum.

Project management becomes a significant issue. How do you balance the ongoing needs for features with a demand for stability? Existing customers have different concerns from new customers.

Crufty code has accumulated, and motivation may be waning. Small features become increasingly problematic as nobody wants to touch the zombie code. Libraries have been deprecated or lost all active maintainers. Or worse, the vendor has removed an essential feature.

How do you deal with turnover in the development teams? How many manual steps are still involved in gathering assets and deploying a new package? How much information was lost with the people that left?

If the product is selling well, you get to face the issue of scalability. I can assure you that whatever plans you had for this will fail on you. Things have to change to adapt to whatever features the users are using most. More than code, the whole organization has to adjust to handle an increasing customer base. There is a lot of stress in growing.

Yet, you still need to start new projects and do small things. Long term projects have the problem of becoming inflexible. New projects give you a chance to try new technology. They remind you of all those small problems that the mature software has long since fixed, or simply ignored. You have a chance to update all your paradigm knowledge and jump on the current programming bandwagon.

Practice requires effort. You can't stick only with your day-to-day work and expect to get better. You must target the things you wish to improve, and branch into new areas.

Practice and experiment. Never stop.

LANGUAGE AND TECHNOLOGY

Computer language design is just like a stroll in the park. Jurassic Park, that is.

— LARRY WALL

*M*uch of your practice will feel like trying to keep up. Instead of learning fun new things, you may get the feeling you're barely escaping irrelevance. All those libraries you learned last decade, or even last year, don't appear to be used anymore. What's with all these new languages people are using. What happened? I took a lunch break, got back and I'm not allowed to use SQL anymore!

There are several ways to look at this problem.

Technology doesn't become irrelevant nearly as fast as it seems. There are a lot of trending things that catch the headlines, but the old stuff isn't disappearing overnight. Talk with programmers on mature projects, and they'll keep recommending older technologies over new ones. Sometimes it's because they're old curmudgeons, but even those fluent in new tech will recommend mature tools. As long there is still an active, engaged, community for a technology, tool, language, or otherwise, it's probably still safe to use.

Fragmentation is more of a problem than obsolescence. Unique tools and technologies evolve for various market segments. The same feature may appear in different forms, or with different capacities. For example, one database may require separate indexes to be created, whereas another database marks fields as searchable. They're both exposing a similar functionality differently, and is often the case, using different terminology.

This pattern repeats through all libraries. Two web stacks necessarily solve the same problem of providing a web service, yet can go about it in seemingly different ways. If we can get by the differences, we can adapt to either approach. We don't lose our abstract knowledge of web stacks just because we're using new technology.

There's a lot of this core programming knowledge that transfers readily. Recruiters make a big deal about knowing specific technologies, but it can get a bit silly. Experienced programmers may never have heard about Technology X, but can learn it in a few days, be productive in a few more, and proficient in a few weeks to a month. The ideas in programming are not changing nearly at the rate the tools are.

Though, the ideas are changing slowly. Even stripped of all the specific tools, the core ideas of programming are dynamic. If you completely ignore trends, you will miss out. It's not hard though. The problematic part is stripping new ideas of their marketing speak and relating them to existing approaches. Nothing is truly new and can be understood as an evolution from existing knowledge.

HOLISTIC PROGRAMMING

Learn not to add too many features right away, and get the core idea built and tested.

— LEAH CULVER

*E*verything is code.
There is no clear division between a library, a language, or external component. As all our tools have grown in complexity and flexibility, it's no longer reasonable to strictly classify the domains of each. In particular, the lines between server administration and software development have radically shifted.

The modern view on software systems, often called "DevOps," is that everything is code. The configuration of your database is in the same class as the language code that accesses it. The load balancer configuration is committed to source control. Deploying new versions is an automated process, stored as versioned scripts. Installing a microservice is no different than installing a library.

This view makes a lot of sense. The pieces are intimately related, and a change in one typically requires a change in the other. A version of one must be matched by a version of the other. Even if a component could be replaced, it's never a one-sided swap.

This approach isn't only about configuration management. It's about changing the view of roles. We stop dividing responsibilities between admins and coders. It's a recognition that the software system must be seen as a whole entity, not a golem cobbled together at the edges.

In the classic view, a database was a prime example of a separate component. The coders wouldn't work on the database, that would have a dedicated database administrator. They'd take care of making sure the database worked, while the coders used it. Even then, it was a dubious distinction. A database isn't something that is "used," a database needs to be configured and coded. Not all tables and queries can be treated the same. The non-database software relies on specific ways in which the database works. Strictly separating the concerns led to contention between teams.

The modern view is that configuration for the database must be managed alongside the code that uses it. A coder is free to modify both sides at once. It increases responsibility but improves overall reliability.

I'm not saying you can't have dedicated administrators. Some people are more drawn to that side of the equation. But they shouldn't be wholly separated from language source code. Many configurations need to make changes in multiple components. An admin should not be artificially limited in the pieces they can modify.

Unfortunately, this approach has issues with human resource management. It's unrealistic to expect that all programmers work on the entire spectrum of a system. For practical reasons, as teams grow, we need to separate people somehow. How precisely these teams work together is an open question. It relies heavily on automation, including testing and deployment.

It creates a question of responsibility. If no team is the owner of a part of the system, does anybody feel actively responsible for its performance? This is a significant perception challenge that must be overcome.

Despite these challenges, the benefits of treating configuration and code as the same are immense. Every push in that direction improves the quality of a system. It's not something that can be ignored for the benefit of simpler HR. All developers need to be working together on the same product. You can see how this is a common theme to my writing.

It's not appropriate to have one part of the system treated as code and the rest not. All of the pieces work together. The entire host, or cluster, configuration is subject to version control, testing, and deployment. The rest of the system sees the host as a single service, not a collection of programs.

AUTOMATION

Each thing you don't have to care about is like a tiny superpower. It frees your brain for other things, and widens your options.

— JESSICA KERR

*I*f the first thing a coder writes is "Hello, World," then the second thing is a script to build it.

Producing software involves an inordinate number of steps. From building, to packaging, to deploying, there's just too much to remember. Even if you can remember the steps, or write them down, it takes too long to do manually. Plus, despite our best intentions, we will make mistakes.

Automation is the key solution to these problems. Not only does it free us from a lot of manual work, but it also doesn't forget things over time. It additionally serves as a great form of documentation. There's no question about what steps are involved, they are written directly in code.

To some, automation may be about reducing workload. But it goes further than that. It's about eliminating redundant effort, freeing us to do the interesting work. Hitting the same sequence of keys, day after day, doesn't help anybody. It's demotivating and terrible for productivity. It's also bad for quality. Manual processes allow steps to be skipped, or forgotten. Automation ensures nothing is omitted. Any additional test or improvement is added long-term. Quality improves over time, rather than degrading.

Unfortunately, there are limits, as some things are difficult to automate. The cost of automation may end up significantly more than the manual effort over the entire life of the project. Again though, the purpose of automation isn't just to save time. It's quite often these difficult to automate pieces which have a high level of manual error. It's usually worth it to automate tricky steps, even if it doesn't save time.

As lovely as automation is, we can't overlook manual oversight. Some steps are best controlled by humans. These are often decisions about when, and which, scripts to execute. We'd additionally want a person to oversee what is happening. Automated processes aren't infallible. It'd be foolhardy to schedule a system upgrade at midnight and not have anybody watching that it goes smoothly.

People remain as amazing problem solvers, whereas scripts are mindless workers. Automation helps free the mind of the developers, letting them watch for real problems, rather than babysit the computers.

VERSION CONTROL

Everything changes and nothing stands still.

— HERACLITUS

ode isn't static. Features are added. Defects are fixed. We need a way to manage the changes sanely. Version control keeps multiple versions of the code as well as a history of the changes.

This isn't a concept unique to code. Word processors have tracked changes for a long time now. It's also not uncommon for graphic artists to save multiple copies of their work. Version control for code follows the same idea. We want to track the changes people have made and compare different versions of the code. Programming has invested heavily in this area looking for good solutions.

Version control serves multiple purposes:

- Allows independent work on the code base. Individuals can work on different features or defects without stumbling over each other.
- Allows changes to be reviewed before merging: when they

become part of the main code. It'll also say when two people have modified the same code, and you need to reconcile it.

- Maintains multiple versions of the software. It's common to support older versions of software with security fixes, while a new version is already available. You may also make new releases available early to beta testers.
- Aids in debugging when a regression defect is introduced. By reviewing what has changed between version, you can hone in on the problem.
- Provides rollback, to revert changes that introduced undesired defects. When something does go wrong, you always have the option of going back to an earlier working version.
- Track the origin and purpose of changes. Author information is recorded for files and lines, as well as linking back to issues that prompted the change.

Most of these purposes can be achieved with a minimal code management process. Difficulty arises as teams grow, and repositories split. Like the code itself, the process will continually change to adapt to maturing software.

I'm going to bring up DevOps here again. The code that is being stored in version control includes language code, automation scripts, tests, and configuration files. The purposes listed above apply to all of these pieces.

CLEAN CODE AND REFACTORING

Any fool can write code that a computer can understand. Good programmers write code that humans can understand.

— MARTIN FOWLER

*Y*ou'll often hear that code is written for other people, not the computer. While not strictly true, there is value in this statement. It's easy to get caught up in the immediate problem while coding. We try one thing, then another. If we assessed coding on how the source changed, it might look like little tornados coming and going.

While it usually solves the problem, the source is left in a bit of disarray. Whatever. It works. Check it in and move on. Two weeks later you come back to the code and have no idea what's going on. This jumble, which made sense before, is undecipherable now.

Code is not a static thing, but a living creature. You'll always come back to code you wrote before and need to modify it. Either you'll need to add a new feature or fix a defect. There's no such thing as perfection and I 100% guarantee the code has issues in it.

Clean code is the idea that we need to write for programmers as well as for the machine. If anything, the needs of reading the code usually outweigh the need for the computer to understand. Compilers are clever things and have come a long way. The need for obscure trickery is relegated to ever smaller corners of computing.

Beyond writing code for us to read, we need to regularly clean up the code. This is called refactoring. We take some code and change how it's written without affecting the functionality. We're taking a purposeful step of making it easier to read, easier to modify and extend.

Ignoring the cleanliness of code will lead to unmaintainable code long term. We can't keep packing in new features, and hacking in quick fixes and expect it to hold together. We must spend time improving the code.

At the same time, we can't be aiming for perfection. Any piece of code, regardless of how pristine you think it is, can be improved. Refactoring has to be prioritized like anything else.

I dissent from a prevailing opinion of refactoring code right after completing a given task or feature. I prefer doing this before adding new features. This approach ensures I'm only ever refactoring code that I need to work on. It answers the question of planning as well. I'm not requesting refactoring time, I'm merely doing it as part of my regular workflow. I think this is how it should be seen as well. It's not a distinct task item, but part of any coding task.

You should be continually refactoring and striving to write clean code.

DEFENSIVE PROGRAMMING

If you want work well done, select a busy man; the other kind has no time.

— ELBERT HUBBARD

*D*efensive programming is about not making assumptions. If you're writing a function, you don't assume the arguments you get are valid. Anything you expect to be true has to be explicitly checked. Rather than assuming a number is in range, you explicitly check it. Rather than assuming something is not null, you check it or use a type that doesn't allow null. If you need an output list to be empty, you test its size. You leave nothing up for question.

Coding in this fashion improves quality. Instead of getting confusing runtime errors, or undefined behaviour, your code produces clear error messages. Debugging becomes a lot easier. The location of the problem is immediately identified along with what the problem is. Furthermore, the code is easier to read: These checks document the expectations of the function -- as opposed to a comment, which may grow outdated.

One step beyond checking the input is handling unexpected input.

A lot of invalid conditions can be made valid with minimal changes in the code. These could be new pathways for empty collections or handling of negative values. Or perhaps a function's return already carries failure information, such as a DB lookup that fails. Unifying error handling with questionable arguments reduces special cases.

Type systems play an active role here. The less specified a value is, the more defensive your code has to be. This isn't to say strongly typed languages are automatically defensive, there are always some more checks that can be done.

Of enormous value is defining custom types that cannot be invalid. It's easier to code defensively if some values cannot be wrong. These aren't assumptions but coded directly into the type. For example, you may have a text template. In the factory or constructor of the type, you parse the template, raising an error if it's invalid. This saves users of the template from worrying about validity. A template instance is always valid.

Whereas clean coding is a bit subjective, defensive coding can be approached rigorously. For any value, we can enumerate all the requirements of that value. As you code this way, you'll learn to see the potential problems, before they ever make it to production.

TESTING

You can control two things: your work ethic and your attitude about anything.

— ALI KRIEGER

*Y*ou won't know if your code works unless you test it.

Testing is a form of quality control that prevents defects from reaching the user. Nobody wants to deal with broken software. It's aggravating, can cause a loss of time and money, and in some cases lead to death.

As a programmer, you won't be the only person testing your software, but you are the first in line. Dedicated testers get just as annoyed as users at obvious and simple defects. It's also shameful to release a new feature only to find out it doesn't work at all. So, to repeat, you are the first person who should test the code you write.

As code evolves, it's important to keep testing it. This gave rise to automated tests. Instead of testing something by hand, once, you write unit tests. These are run regularly, ensuring things that worked before, keep working. A suite of tests enables continuous integration, where code can be regularly merged to the main branch without fear that it breaks.

Some programming methods make testing their highest priority. Test-driven development says you should write the unit tests first, then the code that implements them. The goal is to ensure all new features are tested. Opinions vary, and there are a lot of reasons to diverge from this approach, but the principle is sound. At a more general level, it becomes behaviour, or use, driven development. It's important to test that requirements work, especially the functional requirements.

Automation won't cover everything, nor should it. Most software requires human testers that will manually evaluate the product. It should be no surprise that a sentient being is amazingly good at spotting things which are wrong. People can often be far more efficient, cheaper, and more correct, at performing some kinds of tests, especially when visuals are involved. The division between automated and manual testing is both a technical and management decision.

Manual testing doesn't mean throwing a product into a room full of testers. No, the software needs to be written to be testable for people, just as it needs to be written to be unit tested. The program can have special hooks and debug interfaces for the testers. Often an assisted test program is beneficial, where a combination of automation and human input work together.

Testing won't discover all problems. It's one tool among many you should learn to use, and learn when to use it.

HOW A COMPUTER WORKS

The Analytical Engine weaves algebraic patterns, just as the Jacquard loom weaves flowers and leaves.

— ADA LOVELACE

*A*t one time, it was obvious that a programmer should know how a computer works. Yet, now there are many entry points to the profession that don't require this knowledge. One can get by without really knowing what's going on, but that doesn't seem like a strong position to have. It's good to know the parts of a computer, how memory and CPUs work, how networks communicate, and the whole gamut of hardware level knowledge. If you don't have this knowledge, you'll essentially be playing with magic instead of making informed choices.

Many of the choices about architecture relate to how computers work at their core. There's a significant number of things we don't do because our computers can't do them efficiently. Many other less-than-ideal stuff we do because our computers can do them efficiently.

The core algorithms that make software work all depend on how computers work. The top layers of software may be abstract, but even the first libraries you touch will already be relying on low-level knowledge.

This same knowledge can be applied at higher levels. It lets you understand potential paradoxes. Like why reducing item size is often more efficient than lowering the time complexity of an algorithm. Or why adding more threads can slow a program down. It illuminates the difference between low-level optimization, which you generally should avoid, and high-level data optimization, which you should always do.

If you need more incentive, always think that criminals know how a computer works. Those guys trying to break into your system, steal your users, or take over. Their exploits are based on intimate knowledge of how computers and software really work. Unless you have at least some passing knowledge, you'll neither understand what they do nor have a chance to block them.

You

The human spirit must prevail over technology.

— ALBERT EINSTEIN

*P*rogramming is hard. It's going to be hard on you.
You're going to be the single biggest obstacle to your career. Programming doesn't have a reputation as a calm profession. It's a volatile, competitive industry. But if you handle yourself well, it can be gratifying.

You need to manage your perceptions of yourself. Whether you'd like to follow a process, like the personal software process, track your progress with online coding sites, or set yourself goals, you need to know what you want to get out of your career. You need to learn the abilities required to achieve your goals.

If you can find a good mentor, then great. They can be a valuable source of inspiration, and give guidance on what to do next. You can meet in person, or just chat online. They're there to help you navigate the open fields of programming. You may unfortunately not find one, or discover they aren't for you.

Perhaps you'll find an online community helpful. You're not the only programmer out there. There are millions of us, all at different stages in our career. While many may be focused on the coding side of programming, there are several open to all of development, and even open to helping you specifically. Don't be afraid to try non-programming forums as well. A lot of our problems are shared across roles.

Ultimately this is about you, and you have to discover what works best. Everybody is different, so don't expect to follow a template to success.

That said, there are challenges that we all face.

- Feeling like you don't belong with impostor syndrome
- The stress of working at a company
- Unique stresses from technically challenging work

- Measuring your abilities and progress
- Maintaining productivity and context switching
- Integrating new members into the team
- Surviving the interview process

IMPOSTOR SYNDROME

Being idealistic really helps you overcome some of the many obstacles put in your path.

— ANDY HERTZFELD

Great. You've made it. You've landed a job and been handed a task. You're excited to start working. You sit down the next day and suddenly feel bad. You look at what you've done, and it's all wrong. You're doubting yourself, and questioning why you were even given this task? Is somebody trying to prove that you're no good?

Calm down. Your head is spinning from something known as impostor syndrome. It's a feeling where you doubt your own accomplishments and abilities. You're not alone; 70% of people feel this way at least once.

The stresses of a programming job can do this to you. You're in a new environment, with new faces, tools, and ideas. You read blogs and listen to podcasts about all this cool stuff other people are doing. You see the debates and think everybody is making good points. Add in some out-of-job stresses, and you have an excellent recipe for impostor syndrome.

There are many ways of dealing with this. First, is understanding the stresses you'll face, and find a way to judge your own self-worth. Reading this book is a good start to know how far you've come. It's by no means an easy problem to resolve. Perhaps key is understanding you aren't alone and that there are numerous resources for support.

Don't let your feelings go unchecked. Impostor syndrome can unfortunately become a reality in some situations. What may only be feelings of inadequacy, may become real productivity blockers. This can lead to a cycle of worsening feelings and performance. Even though you're good at programming, you may end up struggling. Do not sit silently and struggle.

Team leads and managers must understand impostor syndrome. You don't want your new team members floundering with negative feelings. As a start, try encouraging team members, and reminding them of their abilities. It can be helpful for them to overcome their concerns. It doesn't even take much effort. A few words throughout the day, or week, can go a long way in making people feel better.

TYPICAL STRESSES

Adopting the right attitude can convert a negative stress into a positive one.

— HANS SELYE

*D*on't lose sight of the fact that programming is a job. However you love it or are drawn to it, you'll end up doing this as a job, in a company.

Being a programmer doesn't shield you from the corporate world. There's no avoiding HR. You have to fill in vacation days, call in sick days, and participate in corporate retreats like everybody else. Accounting will be issuing your pay slips and approving your budgets. Upper-management will be a constant vision -- they should be, it's their job to reflect the company as a whole. You'll have to interact with all of these people.

Plus, you'll want to do this. I said before that I considered everybody in a software company to be a developer. If you're going to adequately represent all these people in the code, you need to communicate with them somehow. The company doesn't exist to support the programmers. You're all part of a team to serve the users.

People being people though, don't share the same opinions. You can have good days and have bad days. We aren't machines, and we are incapable of separating our private life from our work life. I'm adverse to companies that suggest you do -- keeping a rock-solid work/life split seems as detrimental as no split at all. There needs to be a balance. But that means the personal lives, and emotions, of individuals, come to work with them.

All those horror stories you've heard, or read, can happen to you. Working in a company can be stressful, some more than others.

It's of course not all bad. There are many positives. All those people that create stress can also make the day enjoyable. You'll be faced with opportunities you wouldn't have on your own. Lots of good things can happen, so long as you manage to deal with the stress.

Don't lose focus on the user. That's the high-level business goal. You're primarily responsible for the code, but this doesn't mean the code defines the company. Accept and embrace your role, and fight the demons as they come.

UNIQUE STRESSES

You might not think that programmers are artists, but programming is
an extremely creative profession. It's logic-based creativity.

— JOHN ROMERO

*P*rogramming, like many jobs, comes with a set of its own
particular stress points.

Foremost of these are technical issues. These can range from an
infuriating code defect to a cloud service not behaving correctly.
Before getting frustrated, know there are ways to address it. There are
places to get help. But it is easy to get absorbed in the problem and
shut out the world.

A small problem, if it persists for a long time, can demotivate you.
Worse, it may attack your self-worth. If you already suffer from
imposter syndrome, a difficult to fix bug can become a significant
personal issue.

It's vital to find productive ways to deal with the stress of coding.
You won't always have the chance to pass on a problem. Often you
won't be able to find an answer online. Getting anxious, demotivated,
or depressed won't help anybody.

Programming requires a good amount of creativity. Finding workable solutions from a myriad of options isn't a straightforward task. There is no one correct way to solve a problem. We expect programmers to be clever and imaginative. Yet people don't manifest this ability in the same way. For some it's the ultimate source of joy and enumerating solutions comes easily. Others can get stuck and frustrated.

These stresses are not about people, but about our own thoughts. We're wrangling our mind into a certain problem-solving state. As we get deeper, more of our active brain becomes dedicated to the task. Some of us require quiet to do this. I require music. Others need to stare out through the window. Many choose coffee or cola, or perhaps even little squishy toys on their desk.

Whatever your solution is, be aware that technical problems can be difficult. And as much as I say communication is important, you will be faced with tasks that you really need to tackle alone, or possibly in a small insider group. How you deal with this type of stress is a deciding factor in how far you'll advance in your career.

TRACK YOUR OWN PROGRESS

A creative man is motivated by the desire to achieve, not by the desire
to beat others.

— AYN RAND

*T*here's no universal gauge to measure the abilities of a
programmer. Ask anybody who's done interviewing.
They'll tell you it's hard to measure. It can be hard to judge even base-
line abilities, assuming we even know what those are.

There are many aspects to being a programmer. Many of the soft
skills are hard to test. Many of the technical skills aren't good indica-
tors of success. We don't know for sure what combination of abilities
is needed to fill a given position. Clearly, if you have all of the skills I
mention you'll be a good pick. But it'd also be nice to get a job with
less than 20 years of experience.

On the technical side, there is an inordinate number of different
products. It almost feels like luck if you find people using the same
one, or a job listing for specifically what you're good at. Furthermore,
each project has different challenges and different team members. You
may do thrive in one environment and falter in another.

The abilities of a person don't necessarily line up with years of experience either. Not all people develop at the same rate. Not all people have jobs that give them the option to try new things. There'll always be people ahead of you, and always people behind you. You have to decide for yourself where you are going in your career.

Specific technologies can fade quickly, as will your knowledge about them. Yet, there is a lot of programming knowledge that doesn't fade away. This is the type of knowledge that I'm addressing in this book. There are things we can improve on, and get better at, that are independent of a specific platform.

There is no definitive yardstick for this abstract knowledge.

You'll have to rely a bit on faith that you are improving. This is, of course, assuming you're doing targeted practice: work those things you aren't good at. Don't believe you're getting better solely because you have a job in the field.

CONTEXT SWITCHING AND PRODUCTIVITY

What one programmer can do in one month, two programmers can do in two months.

— FRED BROOKS

*Y*ou're almost there, juggling the bits of code in your head. The issue has been tracked, and you've unraveled the mystery. You've jotted a few notes on paper and have some windows open. Your fingers alternate between mouse, keyboard, pen, and fidget toy. Your brain is a glue holding all the bits together...

You get a tap on the shoulder. Somebody had requested your help. Your juggling fails and all the bits you're holding fall apart. It takes only a moment to help the person, but it'll take a while to get back to where you were.

From real people talking to you, to chat messages, to meetings, there's always something that'll come interrupt your day. While some people thrive in multitasking, the majority do not. This isn't solely a programming problem, but a people problem. Most people have jobs that require some thought time. Interruptions can hurt productivity. If the problem goes unchecked, it will hurt morale.

If you didn't skip the first part of this book, you'll recall that programming is about communication. There is no way to avoid it.

Yet, interruptions are at odds with needing quiet time to work on problems.

Any attempt to reduce communication, or isolate the programmers, will fail. You need to find a way to control conversations. I've never seen generalized quiet times work, but providing quiet spaces is an option. Having impromptu meeting rooms available is also beneficial.

An ideal environment has many considerations. It must consider the arrangement of people working, both in the open, discussing things, and privately. The corporate culture must be aware of the need to communicate, yet understand the need for thinking time. Individuals must also practice dealing with context switching. Most of all, everybody needs to be flexible and have a bit of empathy.

NEW TEAM MEMBERS

Team spirit spurs me on. I've always found it easier to be strong for other people than for myself.

— CHERYL COLE

*T*he newbie. Your first job. Each new project. You'll be the new person often. Maybe it'll be a new team, or integrating into an existing one. Each carries its own set of challenges.

Now, try to remember everything you go through. Soon enough there'll be somebody new joining your team. They'll go through a similar set of problems.

Integrating people into teams is difficult. There's a load of knowledge they must acquire before becoming somewhat productive. There's even more they must learn before becoming good team members.

It's a time of conflicts. New members are hired because the existing team has run out of time. This automatically creates stress as it's hard for those current members to spend time with the new hire. Yet it must be done. Otherwise, the newbie will fail at their position.

This is a point where you'll be happy for all the automation you wrote. Pointing newcomers at high-level steps gives them a quick path to productivity. It also provides a clear avenue for learning more -- by digging through the automation scripts.

Onboarding documents can help in growing companies or those with regular turnover. These are good to introduce newcomers to the corporate culture, the general HR and company assets. It may give some idea of the development practice but will lack specifics.

When it gets to a specific project, I've never seen documentation play a significant role. A mentor-student relationship is the most productive. Some teams assign formal mentors, which I consider great. Others default to the team lead. Some make it clear that anybody can be asked. It's best to be formal and clear, as not all people are comfortable asking random people for help. A first line of contact could then introduce them further.

INTERVIEWING

Failure will never overtake me if my determination to succeed is strong enough.

— OG MANDINO

*I*t's unfortunate, but interviews are a slice of chaos. You'll encounter an unfathomable range of styles, abilities, and attitudes in the interview process. Some interviews will provide stellar feedback and be incredible experiences. Others will leave you feeling awful, and questioning your decision to be a programmer.

Navigating this minefield is its own distinct skill.

Recall where I talked about algorithms and complexity theory? They seem to be heavily targeted by some interviewers. This is of questionable value, but if you want to pass the interview, you'll have to practice. Thankfully, there are many sites online that have gamified this.

As a team lead, I have done a lot of interviews. More recently, I've been conducting interviews professionally. I've seen all sorts of things that candidates do wrong, and also right. My interviews tend to have an uncommon but effective style.

If you encounter an interview like mine, you'll need to write a small program from scratch. This may not sound difficult, but most of your experience may be working on existing code bases. The ability to start from scratch is essential to passing interviews. I've done some interviews that extended this into coding mini-projects, which covers a lot more skills but is a much heavier time investment.

Even if you're pressed for time, don't abandon your coding principles. Writing clean code helps the interviewer understand your code. It demonstrates that you can write good code, as opposed to throwing together a rough solution. Your code reveals a great deal about you, your development, where you worked, and your attitudes.

Silence is a big killer in an interview. If the interviewer has no idea what you're thinking, they can't help you. If you're standing in front of people coding, then it's meant to be an interactive experience. Talk about your ideas, and don't be afraid to ask questions. Doing this the right way can get you smoothly through even the toughest of questions.

And breathe. Remain calm and try to be a pleasant person. Your personality is as much on review as your technical skills. Nobody wants to work with somebody who is unpleasant. Nobody wants to work with somebody who gets overly stressed.

This goes both ways. Be sure to assess the people interviewing you. You can learn a great deal about a company from how they conduct interviews. You want to avoid a lousy environment.

For your own health, don't fret the misses. Like any skill, it takes time to develop your interviewing. The more interviews you do, the better you'll get at it. Even then, sometimes it just isn't the right fit with the company. Sometimes you're just having a bad day, or the interviewer is.

MOVING FORWARD

*T*hat's a lot.

Programming is a rich field. There are enough areas of interest to keep you busy through your entire career.

You may not like all of the things I mentioned, but that doesn't negate their relevance. You may even find jobs that don't require all of these skills, or ones where they try to specialize the roles. What you'll discover though, is that the more of these skills you have, the better you'll perform in any of the roles.

Programming is a modern occupation, and how we interact with others is still in flux. The technology we're using is rapidly changing. The approach to our work is still hotly debated. This makes it an exciting field, yet creates a high burden of knowledge. You need to know a lot to be a good programmer. You need both solid technical and people skills to become a great programmer.

Don't get frustrated though, as none of this will come overnight. As you work, and practice, you'll grow in all areas I've covered in this book. While some of the topics can be actively studied, other skills come only from experience. With my further books, I'm hoping I can jump-start that experience, and help you find new areas of interest.

I'd like to make this an interactive effort. I didn't learn in a vacuum, nor should you. What I know is rightfully attributed to all the great people I've worked with over the years. I'm always happy to learn from new people, and help them learn in turn. So please contact me saying what you'd like to have covered, what you think could be improved, or to start a dialog.

Stay informed of upcoming books by subscribing to my mailing list:

edaqa.com/read/programming

Thank you for reading. I look forward to supporting you in your programming career.

Made in the USA
Middletown, DE
26 March 2019